The Sacred Book
of
Theories

By Jervon L Salters

Table of Contents

Why I Wrote This Book

I wrote this book to contribute to society and to offer guidance to those who are struggling to find their way. The state of the world we live in concerns me deeply, and I believe that we need to come together and face the challenges we encounter. The words in this book are meant to provide wisdom, much like a loving father would pass down to his family. This book is for anyone who wants to improve themselves and their lives, young men in and out of prison, individuals who are about to give up, and those who have been misled by society. My hope is that this book can be a source of inspiration for anyone at a crossroad, or those who may be committed to the wrong path.

Are These Really Theories?

The Theories I have developed are based on a combination of personal experiences, stories shared by elders in my community, and observations. Initially, I verbally utilized my stories as a means of imparting knowledge of the overarching lesson. However, I found that many individuals would forget the story when attempting to convey the lessons to others. Consequently, it was requested that I put my insights in writing. Given the length of the stories, I created these theories. While some may question the validity of these theories, I invite them to use that energy to disprove and debate them. I have discovered that energy is a proven tool that can be utilized in the pursuit of knowledge. Overall, I encourage you to enjoy these theories.

Dedication

This book is dedicated to my family, both present and past. As a young man, I felt like I was born into society's ditch. I didn't have the basic necessities, and I sought ways to fill the void. I tried turning to my home, but that didn't work. So, like many others, I reached out to society for answers. Unfortunately, many of our communities are broken, and those in power have compromised the people we idolize. To feel good about ourselves, we do what we can - we hide our insecurities behind our clothing, cars, possessions, and now, more than ever, behind our phones. As a society, we lack exposure and are just actors playing out shallow roles. What we need is positive exposure to build our core, so we can be okay. When a man is broken, his family is exposed to "The world".

Youth Theory

A kid is a clean slate, they gain information from the environment they were born into. You must expose them to a variety of positive individuals, opportunities, and outcomes for them to follow. The core to the youth theory is exposure "if you can see it, you could become it" we are all actor to life's scripts.

You're Not Always Right Theory

It is common for people to become upset when someone uses logic, especially when it contradicts their beliefs or opinions. While everyone makes mistakes and no one is perfect, using logic and wisdom should not be punished. In fact, using logic and wisdom is often the best way to approach a situation. It allows for a more objective and rational assessment of the facts, which can lead to a better outcome. When someone tells you that you are not always right, it is important to remind him or her that they are not always wrong.

Distraction Theory

Distraction Theory refers to anything that hinders, obstructs, or slows down progress, growth, or a positive movement. It doesn't matter whether the barrier is intentional or unintentional; what's important is the fact that it halts your progress towards your goals. Such hindrances could be something as minor as getting a phone call while watching a self-help video on YouTube, or something as severe as someone deliberately plotting against you to remove you from their path.

The Power Of Praise Theory

The Power of Praise theory suggests that we possess the remarkable ability to positively impact the lives of others through the simple act of recognizing their unique qualities or expressing faith in their potential. By acknowledging what makes them special or by believing in their future success, we can inspire and uplift those around us. This theory has been tested and proven to be effective in fostering personal growth and development.

Must Be Nice Theory

The phrase "must be nice" is often used sarcastically, implying that the person being addressed has something that the speaker does not. It can also be a way for people to display their envy in a thinly-veiled compliment. If you've ever used this phrase, think about how you felt when you said it - chances are, there was some underlying resentment or jealousy.

Procrastination Theory

The Procrastination Theory states that delaying a task creates opportunities for obstacles to arise. Instead, if the task is essential, we should aim to complete it as soon as possible or at the next available option. Just like a tree grows when it has all the necessary resources, we should act instantly and not delay growth.

Destruction Theory

Destruction Theory explains how societal and environmental factors can affect a person's ability to succeed. When everything around a person contributes to failure, it creates a negative environment that makes it difficult to find solutions. Popular culture and societal norms can promote activities that lead to destruction. People in power may not want others to achieve their full potential as it could threaten their authority. They may be content with individuals never reaching their peak because it prevents them from becoming a potential threat.

Stranger Theory

According to the stranger theory, when you meet someone new, they are often more willing to share their experiences and knowledge with you than the people they already know. This is because they don't perceive you as a threat or competition. Instead, they view meeting new people as an opportunity to showcase their gains, accomplishments, and the roadmap to their success. Meeting strangers is especially beneficial when you are not where you want to be in life and want to explore new possibilities.

The True Attraction Theory

When a man has reached full maturity, he understands his role in society, is confident in himself, and possesses intelligence. At this stage, it becomes "almost impossible" for him to develop a platonic friendship with a single woman who is also at a stage in her life where she is seeking a companion. Similarly, for a fully developed woman, it is difficult to maintain a purely friendly relationship with a man. The natural attraction between men and women is bound to surface, provided there are no other inhibiting factors.

The Cotton Theory

The Cotton Theory is a powerful reminder that our past does not define us, but rather serves as a source of inspiration for creating a brighter future. By looking to history, we gain valuable insight into the struggles, challenges, and triumphs of our ancestors, and we can use this knowledge to shape our own lives and the lives of those we care about. We must strive to achieve what our forebears were unable to, while also honoring their sacrifices and keeping their memory alive. By doing so, we can ensure that our loved ones and we will never have to endure the hardships and injustices that were once an everyday reality for those who picked cotton.

The Direction Theory

The Direction Theory advises individuals to question the status quo and consider alternative paths, especially when everyone else is following the same direction. This theory highlights the tendency of people to blindly follow trends without proper research, leading to missed opportunities and poor decisions. Therefore, the theory suggests taking a more thoughtful approach, being willing to think critically, do research, and trust one's instincts. By venturing down new paths, we can broaden our horizons and discover new opportunities that we would have otherwise missed.

The Garden Theory

People often ignore an important message simply because they don't like the messenger. The Garden Theory draws a parallel between the message and a garden. Just like how you don't go to a garden to take everything in it including the snakes, bugs, and vegetables you don't like, but rather only what you desire to eat; similarly, when receiving a message, you shouldn't focus on the messenger and their ways, but rather on the message itself that you can benefit from. Never reject information solely because you dislike the messenger.

Listen With Your Mouth Talk With Your Ears Theory

If you learn to talk with your ears and listen with your mouth, then you've figured out, the key to higher knowledge and understanding. Effective communication involves more than just speaking; it involves active listening as well. By prioritizing listening, you can gain a deeper understanding of others' perspectives and experiences. When you talk with your ears, you can truly absorb what others are saying, which can lead to greater insights and knowledge. Without the ability to talk, you are forced to rely solely on your listening skills, and potentially gaining a deeper understanding of the world around you.

Up One Theory

The Up One Theory is based on the fact that often individuals you have strong relationships with secretly see you as competition. When they move up, or gain a position over you, they either hold you down or do what it takes to maintain a step up on you. They will also make sure they don't share what it took to be in their position because they feel good about just being Up One on You.

The Blessing Theory

The Blessing Theory postulates that individuals may enter our lives for a specific reason, often arising from the hand of destiny, with the intention of either improving our circumstances or saving us from dire situations. When such moments arise, it behooves us to be receptive to these blessings, even if they come from unfamiliar or unexpected sources. Accepting such blessings is integral to our growth and prosperity and can serve as a catalyst for unlocking our full potential.

Fine Print Theory

It is often believed that one can take shortcuts and ignore the fine print, but this only leads to loss of control and regret down the line. By disregarding the opportunity to read the fine print, one is likely to make hasty decisions that will have negative consequences. It is essential to pay attention to the details and understand the terms and conditions before making any decision.

The Window Theory

The concept of Window Theory encapsulates the notion that knowledge is not passive, but rather is something that must be actively sought out and absorbed. It is said that a person who spends their life staring at a wall, even if they double your age, may have acquired less knowledge than a individual who has spent their life looking out the window of life, actively seeking knowledge and experiences. While it's okay to encourage others to seek knowledge and experiences, it's important not to lose oneself in the process of helping them, as some individuals may find comfort in their current state and prefer to keep staring at the wall.

Lion Theory

The Lion Theory is all about taking bold action based on your past experience and unwavering confidence in a situation. This could be a familiar pattern that leads to a predictable outcome or something you've encountered before. You stand your ground and refuse to let anyone alter your thoughts. It's crucial, though, that you're absolutely certain you're right before taking action. Trust in your instincts and act decisively.

Solution Theory

The solution theory simply states that if you can tell your story about your tough upbringing, and the problems of the past, then you survived it. Though you may never forget it or may still feel the pain, it's time to work on a solution. Laying in the misery of the past brings on more stress.

The Gimmick Theory

The Gimmick Theory is based on the idea that people who use illegal means to gain money could simply find a job to justify their assets. However, this is not a smart move, but rather a total gimmick. When the time comes, the money will not be divided, and you will be locked up. The clean and dirty money will be considered as one, just like a cup filled with 50% clean water and 50% sewer water is all sewer water.

Sink Bath Theory

In life often people claim they are going to change their life and move in another direction, but they are in the same environment with the same tools, and ingredients. Just like a person taking a sink bath, the same dirt in the same areas are just being moved around but you think you are going to be fresh and clean. The Sink Bath Theory insists that if you want to be better and clean up your act you must be able to let the dirt go down the drain and rinse away the old ways. You cannot half clean yourself. It is all or none.

Line Theory

According to the Line Theory, if we want to make a change in our lives, we need to be fully committed to our goals and avoid risky or uncomfortable situations. This means that we cannot dislike our current situation or the outcome of our decisions, yet constantly put ourselves in compromising situations by crossing, balancing, or jumping across the line. Therefore, a person who attempts to outwit the line of pain will become a victim of their choices, proving that they are not fully committed.

Problem or Solution Theory

The Problem or Solution Theory came in the form of a question from a young man inquiring about my position on his journey in prison. Daily I would post positive quotes in my office window to promote a positive atmosphere. One day the young man came to me and stated that he had a quote for me. "Are you part of the problem or solution?" This was a powerful question because every individual should ask himself or herself this same question when it comes to their family, job, and/or community. Are you a part of the problem or solution?

Buzzard Theory

It is often stated that individuals should be wary of "crabs in a barrel," as these creatures have a tendency to pull others down and impede their success. However, it is important to consider that the crab is simply trying to escape captivity and return to the freedom it once had. If given the opportunity to climb a ladder, it would climb to the top floor; if the other crabs had strong legs and arms, they would all reach the top. But the crab pulls the others down in an attempt to escape as it grabs what's available. While we may be wary of the crabs in our life, it is the buzzards we should truly fear. These are the individuals who wait for us to stumble and fall, only to pounce on us and feed off our misfortunes. They are the ones who see us at our weakest and use our demise as their meal. It is important to be aware of the buzzards in our life and to protect ourselves from their harmful intentions.

Peace Theory

It's common for us to present our opinions as though they're facts or try to mold others to fit our vision of who they ought to be. However, it's essential to recognize that we cannot force others to change, as they are not our responsibility to fix. If a situation doesn't directly affect us or someone we care about, we should allow others to be themselves. It's possible to offer guidance to someone who exhibits a bad habit we dislike, but it's also natural for life to take its course and deal with the problem. We should learn to pick our battles and refrain from being too quick to judge others, every battle is not your war and every villain is not a part of your script. Embrace peace!

Rollercoaster Theory

In relationships, the rollercoaster theory suggests that the path is more like a rollercoaster than a highway. We often face the same problems and tend to get confused, thinking that they are new. Relationships have their ups and downs, twists and turns, and steep dives, but usually, the underlying issue remains the same. The problem arises when we expect different actions from the same person, and we act like the path is entirely different. Just like a rollercoaster, the path of relationships doesn't go straight, but it goes in circles.

The Venom Theory

The Venom Theory suggests that it is not in a snake's job description to let you know whether it is venomous. It is your responsibility to be aware of the type of snake you are dealing with, or else you run the risk of being bitten by venomous ones. This concept can be applied to life as well. You should always be attentive to your surroundings and cautious of potential hazards. Lack of knowledge can lead to unfavorable outcomes.

The Endless Milk Theory

The endless milk theory suggests that a mother's love for her son can be both a gift and a curse. A mother's love can shield her son from pain, but this can lead to him being unprepared when faced with pain later in life. Like a guitar player, a young man needs to build up calluses to develop thicker skin and better cope with pain. While a mother's love and protection is important, a young man also needs to experience failure and disappointment to learn how to handle pressure and become a mature adult. Ultimately, this will help him become a better partner in future relationships. A mother will always be there to support her son until he is able to be independent, but dependency on her milk can lead to a situation where he is not ready to face the world on his own, leaving him feeling lost and helpless.

The Frame Theory

The Frame Theory is a concept that emphasizes the importance of building a solid foundation for a lasting and healthy relationship. According to this theory, a relationship without a strong frame is like building a doghouse without a frame. If you build a frameless doghouse, it will most likely not last as long as the dog, whereas a framed one will probably outlive it. In the same way, relationships built on material possessions, superficial characteristics, or the perceptions of others are like frameless doghouses that may crumble over time. Such relationships may not survive the challenges and changes that life inevitably brings. Therefore, it is essential to establish a strong foundation based on mutual trust, respect, communication, and shared values.

Jimmy Miller's Buckle Under Theory

There is one conversation I had with my coach that has stayed with me over time. I was once in a situation where I got in trouble despite being innocent and was given group consequences, which I refused to accept. My coach told me he believed me and knew I was telling the truth, but the situation escalated when I continued to argue instead of accepting the light punishment. As a result, I ended up receiving the harshest punishment compared to everyone else. He told me, "Son, sometimes you have to accept defeat instead of risking everything to win it all." He said I needed to learn to buckle under. Unfortunately, I didn't follow his advice and ended up repeating the same grade.

Double Dutch Theory

Double Dutch Theory: Timing is key. Double Dutch is a jump rope style that requires strategic timing to determine when to commence jumping. This concept can be applied to conversations as well. It is imperative to exercise caution and prudence when joining conversations, rather than impulsively interjecting oneself. One must be strategic and only engage in conversations when the timing is appropriate. Failure to do so may result in becoming entangled in a situation for which one is unprepared. Therefore, it is essential to exercise discretion and be mindful of timing when engaging in conversations.

Wake Up Theory

When individuals such as one's mother and grandmother abandon them, it is indicative of being on a misguided path. These are two individuals who will undoubtedly provide unwavering support, and if they both express that they are relinquishing their support, it is a clear indication that the individual's actions and decisions will likely result in an unfavorable outcome. When mamma and granny give up on you, obviously you need to make adjustments.

Clay Theory

According to the concept of clay theory, human beings tend to mold and shape others in accordance with their own desires. This can lead to a situation where individuals fail to recognize and appreciate their true selves and instead feel pressured to constantly alter themselves to meet the expectations of others. The analogy of a sculptor working with a block of clay is often used to describe this phenomenon. Just as a skilled sculptor may not be satisfied with creating just one masterpiece, those with this ability to mold and shape others may also continue to seek out new "creations" to satisfy their desires.

Not My Thing Theory

The "Not my thing Theory" is a common situation where individuals face challenges and struggles in their current position, be it their job, life, or relationship. These individuals may feel unsatisfied, unfulfilled, or unhappy with their current circumstances. However, when presented with a more productive and positive opportunity, they may refuse to take it due to their reluctance to leave their comfort zone, fear of the unknown, or their reluctance to accept your vision and advice.

The Spinning World Theory

The Spinning World Theory is a concept that suggests that life is a continuous cycle of events, much like a spinning wheel. As a child, I was curious about the world and eager to try new things. However, my father used to remind me that everything had been done before and that history often repeats itself. We face numerous obstacles and challenges that test our strength and resilience. If we are not careful, we can easily become overwhelmed and lose our sense of purpose. Through learning from our errors, we can break free from the cycle and reach new heights of achievement .

The Ant Theory

The ant theory is a well-known analogy that highlights the importance of distinguishing between perception and reality. Just because something looks like a cake and smells like a cake, doesn't mean it is a cake. In the same way, life may appear glamorous and full of glitter and gold, but it can be dangerous if you don't do your homework. If you were to put your hands in an ant nest covered in icing thinking it's a cake, you will feel the wrath of those ants, not the sweet taste of a cake. It's crucial to understand that perception may be powerful, but reality is more valuable in the long run.

Your Guy Theory

It's not right to expect me to tolerate someone who disrespects me just because you have learned to accept their behavior. A man with standards won't adjust his day to accommodate your disrespectful friend. Ultimately, it is your responsibility, not mine, to manage your friend and their behavior. I refuse to allow their negative conduct to impact my life, and I will not be making any adjustments to accommodate them. It is imperative to establish clear boundaries and demand respect from individuals in our lives, particularly those who may negatively affect our personal, professional or academic pursuits.

The Plate Theory

The Plate theory is based on the notion of not judging others by their possessions, perceived treatment, or one's own belief of being treated unfairly. It is imperative to understand that we do not know the reason behind their favorable treatment. While some people may be in a position temporarily, they may face negative consequences in the long run. Some may have made sacrifices that we might not be willing to make to earn their position, while others may earn favor because they need special assistance. Therefore, it is essential to avoid comparing one's plate with that of others as it could lead to disappointment. Instead, it is crucial to focus on oneself and work towards personal growth.

World Against Me Theory

The "world against me" theory is a fallacy that one may perceive the world to be persistently antagonistic. This perception, often driven by internal factors, manifests as a sensation of being under constant assault and hindered from achieving success due to several obstacles. The individual may feel overwhelmed and struggle to attain positive outcomes in an environment that appears to be working against their interests. It is imperative to note that this battle occurs internally, and it is essential to find one's place in this vast universe.

Family Section

Uncle Son's Slow Down Theory

Slow down, and you will last longer! Uncle Son's Slow Down Theory is a simple yet essential concept that holds true in various aspects of our lives. The theory suggests that moving too fast can lead to missing crucial details that could make a significant difference in the outcome. More so, when you move too fast, it's easy for others to perceive you as unreliable, which can be detrimental in both personal and professional settings.

Aunt Plummy's Finders Theory

I was about twelve when I looked inside the crease of my aunt's couch and found a dollar. I instantly yelled, yes, I found a dollar. She reached her hand out to take the dollar and told me a valuable lesson, "You can't find things in other people's house, and that it belongs to someone." The money was gone, but the lesson was received.

Uncle Ed's Momma Theory

Uncle Ed once shared that his Momma used to say, "It's more in your head than nit and louse." This phrase encourages people to think critically and make decisions based on their experiences, rather than acting impulsively without considering the consequences. Essentially, it means that it's important to use your brain, be smart and intelligent, and exercise good judgment.

Translation-Louse is the lice and nit is the eggs they lay.

Thanks, Waxie

Took's Gossip Theory

Several years ago my cousin 'Took" was sick and word went around that he might not make it. A week later I pulled up to the gas station and I saw him standing in front of the building, he came to my truck, tapped on the window, I put it down and he asked "Hey! How am I doing" this was his way of saying that he heard through the grape vine that he was down bad. Took dispelled the Gossip by his presence.

Lynn's Perpetrating a Fraud Theory

Often we point the finger at others and propel ourselves by finding issues in others, we attempt to be righteous ignoring our own flaws. We should take Lynn's advice and stop perpetrating a fraud! We all got some nonsense with us, and the people that really know you will eventually call you out on it.

Ciceroe's Consequence Theory

When I was younger, I used to blame others and avoid taking responsibility whenever I found myself in trouble. However, one day, my father taught me a valuable lesson. He told me that I should always make my own decisions because I am the one who must face the consequences, not my friends. He also emphasized that he was the consequence. This message has stayed with me throughout my life, and it has saved me from making many poor decisions. Although I was laughed at for walking away from trouble on some occasions, I am proud that I did. The fear and presence of my father made a huge difference.

Ciceroe's Three Years Give Back 20 Theory

As I was growing up, I always found it fascinating to see guys not much older than myself with fancy cars and expensive jewelry. However, my father always warned me not to be fooled by them, as they were living a fast-paced life that would eventually catch up with them. He used to say that they were trying to fit in 20 years of life in just 2 or 3 years but would eventually have to give back 20 years or even their entire life.

Mr. Murray's People Do According To Their Understanding Theory

Often we see people and we make an instant reaction to their behavior; Mr. Murray theory make us question if this person was ever taught the correct way, did this person have guidance, was they raised the right way. You cannot beat, kill, or turn away everyone that does not act accordingly. You should attempt to teach them, educate them, and show them the right way because people often do according to what they understand as right.

Ma's Trash Theory

I once was upset with my nephew and told my mother that he was trash. She instantly stopped me and said never call anyone trash, everyone got something good about them and no one is trash. She said choose some new words.

Ma's Paused Emotion Theory

When my father passed away, my mother pulled me aside and said, "Hey let's put our tears aside and let's make sure his business was straight." Years later my sister Lynn passed away and my mom was placed in the hospital; I put the tears aside and took care of the business. A few years ago, Covid-19 hit and my mother and I were hospitalized. I got a call while in the hospital from my mom's health care provider early on a Friday morning that my mother had passed! I could not put my tears aside, but I left the hospital that day and started the process of taking care of her business. When I finally saw her at the funeral home, she had a smile on her face. RIP MA

This Theory has many lessons,

- No matter how you feel business must be taken care of.

- A good mother knows what her child can handle.

- Prepare your family for the future.

- Lead by example because someone will follow.

- When momma warns you that this day might be soon listen.

- Finish the mission.

- Make sure momma smiles.

Special Message

A child must be groomed into adulthood, just aging is not enough to move them into their full potential. Often, we are a product of our environment, and we are molded by what we experience within our communities. Although we at times see a rose grow from the concrete, it does not mean that we can grow roses under the concrete. It means that exceptional individuals were able to beat the odds and become a success. My years of experience showed me that exposure is a powerful tool in the development of our youth. Everyone wants to be first at something and we often compete based on what is seen as the only competition but in reality, it is all we have been exposed to and that there are a lot more opportunities available.

Coming Soon

Throw love out the window is as a small guide to use when one makes the major decision to get married. Marriage can be the most beautiful thing in the world that two people can create, however it can also be what can destroy you. Many people in relationships fear **CONFLICT** and **HONESTY** which causes them to deter their wants and needs in order to please each other. Then they use the word **LOVE** as a bond and think that all is good. A person will only hide their true feelings and thoughts for a short period of time. I call this period in the relationship **SHADOW LOVE** . Shadows are weak and when the light hits, it fades away.

Thank you for your purchase.

Jervon Salters

Personal Notes